Dedication

To my incredible children,

This book is dedicated to you, not just as a reflection of my journey, but as a beacon for your own. Watching you grow with a passion for real estate fills me with immense pride and joy. Your aspirations to follow in this path inspire me every day to continue striving for excellence and integrity in all that I do.

May this guide serve as both a resource and a reminder that with dedication, knowledge, and heart, you can achieve anything you set your minds to. The future is yours to shape, and I have no doubt that you will leave a memorable mark on the real estate world.

With all my love and support,

Dad

A Special Thanks

I want to extend my deepest gratitude to the dedicated REALPRO agents from REALPRO International. Your hard work, commitment to excellence, and unwavering support have been instrumental in our shared success. This book is as much a reflection of your efforts as it is of mine. Thank you for being the backbone of this journey and for your continued dedication to helping our clients achieve their dreams of homeownership. Your contributions are truly appreciated, and I am honored to work alongside such a talented and passionate team.

Thank you all for being a part of this journey. Together, we are making a lasting impact.

Table Of Contents

Introduction	**6**
Chapter 1: Understanding Homeownership	**8**
Why Buy a Home?	8
Renting vs. Buying	9
The Benefits of Homeownership	9
Chapter 2: Preparing to Buy a Home	**11**
Assessing Your Financial Health	11
Understanding Credit Scores	12
Saving for a Down Payment	12
Pre-Approval Process	13
Chapter 3: Understanding Your Homebuying Needs	**15**
Defining Your Must-Haves and Nice-to-Haves	15
Considering Location, Size, and Style	16
Making Informed Decisions	17
Chapter 4: Finding the Right Real Estate Agent	**19**
Why Work with a REALPRO Agent?	19
How to Choose the Right Agent	20
The Role of a REALPRO Agent	21
Chapter 5: Navigating the Real Estate Market	**24**
Understanding Market Conditions	24
How to Research Homes and Neighborhoods	25
Visiting Open Houses and Private Showings	27
Chapter 6: Making an Offer	**29**
Understanding Offer Strategies	29
Writing a Strong Offer	30
How Your REALPRO Agent Assists	31
Chapter 7: The Home Inspection	**33**

    Why Inspections Matter   33
    Common Issues Found in Inspections   34
    Negotiating Repairs or Price Adjustments   36

Chapter 8: Securing a Mortgage   **38**
    Understanding Mortgage Options   38
    Choosing the Right Lender   40
    How Interest Rates Affect Your Mortgage   41
    The Role of Your Agent in Mortgage Negotiations   43

Chapter 9: The Appraisal Process   **44**
    What to Expect During an Appraisal   44
    How Appraisals Affect Your Loan   45
    Dealing with Low Appraisals   46

Chapter 10: Preparing for Closing   **49**
    What Happens Before Closing?   49
    Reviewing the Closing Disclosure   51
    Final Walkthrough Checklist   52

Chapter 11: Closing Day   **55**
    Understanding Closing Costs   55
    The Documents You'll Sign   57
    What to Expect During the Closing Meeting   58

Chapter 12: After the Purchase   **60**
    Moving Into Your New Home   60
    Managing Home Maintenance   62
    Understanding Property Taxes and Insurance   63

Chapter 13: Best Practices for Homebuyers   **66**
    Staying Organized Throughout the Process   66
    Common Mistakes to Avoid   68
    How to Communicate Effectively with Your Agent   69

Chapter 14: Real Estate in Different Markets   **72**

Buying in a Seller's Market vs. Buyer's Market	72
Understanding Seasonal Trends	73
Buying a Home in a Competitive Market	75
Chapter 15: Working with REALPRO for Your Next Home	**77**
Selling Your Home with REALPRO	77
REALPRO's Commitment to Customer Satisfaction	79
How REALPRO Supports You in the Long Term	81

Introduction

Homeownership has long been considered a cornerstone of the American Dream—a symbol of stability, success, and personal achievement. Yet, the process of buying a home can be complex, overwhelming, and filled with uncertainties, especially for first-time buyers. As someone who has spent over two decades in the real estate industry, I have witnessed firsthand the challenges that homebuyers face and the immense satisfaction that comes with helping them navigate these challenges to achieve their goals.

This book, *The Ultimate Guide to Homebuying The REALPRO Way!*, was born out of a deep desire to empower homebuyers with the knowledge and confidence they need to make informed decisions. Whether you're taking your first steps toward homeownership, looking to upgrade, or exploring investment opportunities, this guide is designed to demystify the process and provide you with the tools to succeed.

Why is this book important? Because buying a home is not just a financial transaction; it's a life-changing event that can shape your future in profound ways. The decisions you make during this process will affect your finances, your family, and your sense of security for years to come. It's crucial to approach this journey with a clear understanding of each step and the potential pitfalls along the way.

In my career, I've seen many buyers embark on this journey without the necessary guidance, only to encounter avoidable obstacles and setbacks. I believe that with the right information, every buyer can approach the market with confidence, avoid common mistakes, and ultimately find the home that meets their needs and dreams.

This book is more than just a manual—it's a reflection of my commitment to helping people achieve homeownership with clarity and peace of mind. I've taken care to include detailed explanations, practical advice, and relatable examples, drawn from real experiences, to make the content accessible and relevant to a wide audience.

At REALPRO, we are dedicated to supporting our clients not just during the transaction, but throughout their entire homeownership journey. This guide is an extension of that commitment, providing ongoing support and resources that you can return to at any stage of the process.

Homeownership is a significant milestone, and my goal is to make your path to achieving it as smooth and rewarding as possible.

Thank you for allowing me to be a part of your journey. I hope this book serves as a valuable companion as you move forward with confidence toward your new home.

Warm regards,

Eduardo Marines
CEO, REALPRO International

Chapter 1: Understanding Homeownership

Owning a home is a significant milestone in anyone's life, representing both an emotional achievement and a financial investment. For many, the dream of homeownership symbolizes stability, success, and a place to call their own. But what exactly does owning a home entail, and why is it often seen as one of the most important investments a person can make?

Why Buy a Home?

Homeownership offers a range of benefits that renting simply cannot match. When you own a home, you're not just paying for a place to live—you're investing in an asset that can grow in value over time. This growth, known as home equity, is one of the primary financial advantages of owning a home. Equity is the difference between the current market value of your home and what you owe on your mortgage. As you pay down your mortgage and as property values increase, your equity grows, providing you with financial security and the ability to borrow against it if needed.

In addition to the financial benefits, owning a home gives you a sense of permanence and community. Unlike renting, where you may have to move frequently due to lease terms or other factors, owning a home allows you to establish roots in a community. You can get to know your neighbors, participate in local events, and feel more connected to your surroundings.

Renting vs. Buying

The decision between renting and buying is a personal one, but it's essential to weigh the pros and cons carefully. Renting offers flexibility—if you need to move for a job or want to try out different neighborhoods before settling down, renting may be a good option. However, renting also comes with limitations. Rent can increase annually, and you're subject to the landlord's rules and regulations. Additionally, the money you spend on rent each month does not contribute to any future financial gain—it's simply an expense.

Buying a home, on the other hand, is an investment. While it may require a larger upfront cost, including a down payment and closing costs, the long-term benefits often outweigh these initial expenses. For example, let's say you're renting a home for $1,500 per month. Over five years, you'll have paid $90,000 in rent. If you were to purchase a home with a mortgage payment of $1,500 per month, a portion of that payment would go toward paying down the principal of your loan, building equity in your home. After five years, not only would you have a place to live, but you'd also own a portion of that property.

The Benefits of Homeownership

The benefits of homeownership extend beyond just financial gain. Homeowners have the freedom to personalize their space, making changes and improvements as they see fit. Whether it's painting the walls, remodeling the kitchen, or landscaping the yard, you can create a living environment that truly reflects your personality and lifestyle.

Furthermore, homeownership often comes with tax advantages. In many cases, homeowners can deduct mortgage interest and property taxes on their annual tax returns, which can result in significant savings. Over time, these tax benefits can help offset the costs of homeownership, making it more affordable than renting in the long run.

One of the most compelling reasons to buy a home is the sense of stability it provides. Unlike renting, where you may face uncertainty if your landlord decides to sell the property or raise the rent, owning a home means you have control over your living situation. This stability is particularly important for families, as it allows children to grow up in a consistent environment, attend the same schools, and build lasting friendships in the neighborhood.

Owning a home is also a hedge against inflation. As rental prices continue to rise, having a fixed-rate mortgage means your monthly housing costs remain stable, even as the cost of living increases. This predictability can provide peace of mind, knowing that your housing costs won't unexpectedly skyrocket.

Finally, owning a home can be a source of pride and accomplishment. For many, it's the culmination of years of hard work and savings, and it represents a significant life achievement. The feeling of walking into a home that you own, knowing that it's truly yours, is an unparalleled experience.

Chapter 2: Preparing to Buy a Home

Buying a home is a major financial commitment, and preparation is key to ensuring a smooth and successful experience. Before you start searching for your dream home, it's essential to take a close look at your financial situation, understand the homebuying process, and gather the necessary documents. Proper preparation not only helps you avoid potential pitfalls but also puts you in a stronger position to make an offer when you find the right property.

Assessing Your Financial Health

The first step in preparing to buy a home is assessing your financial health. This involves taking a comprehensive look at your income, expenses, debts, and savings. Start by creating a budget that includes all your monthly expenses, such as rent, utilities, groceries, and transportation. Then, compare your total expenses to your monthly income to determine how much you can afford to spend on a mortgage payment.

A general rule of thumb is that your monthly housing costs, including your mortgage payment, property taxes, and insurance, should not exceed 28% to 30% of your gross monthly income. For example, if you earn $5,000 per month before taxes, your total housing costs should be no more than $1,500. This ensures that you have enough income left over to cover other expenses and save for future needs.

Understanding Credit Scores

Your credit score plays a crucial role in determining whether you qualify for a mortgage and what interest rate you'll receive. Lenders use credit scores to assess your creditworthiness, which is a measure of how likely you are to repay your loan. A higher credit score indicates that you have a strong history of managing credit responsibly, while a lower score may suggest that you've had difficulties in the past.

Credit scores range from 300 to 850, with higher scores indicating better credit. Generally, a score of 740 or higher is considered excellent, while a score of 620 or lower may make it more challenging to qualify for a mortgage. If your credit score is lower than you'd like, there are steps you can take to improve it before applying for a mortgage.

Start by checking your credit report for errors, such as incorrect account information or late payments that you can dispute. Paying down high-interest debt, such as credit card balances, can also help boost your score. Additionally, avoid opening new credit accounts in the months leading up to your mortgage application, as this can temporarily lower your score.

Saving for a Down Payment

One of the most significant financial hurdles for many homebuyers is saving for a down payment. A down payment is the amount of money you pay upfront when purchasing a home, typically expressed as a percentage of the home's purchase price. While the traditional down payment amount is 20%, many lenders offer mortgage options that require as little as 3% to 5% down.

For example, if you're purchasing a home for $300,000, a 20% down payment would be $60,000, while a 5% down payment would be $15,000. Keep in mind that a lower down payment often means higher monthly mortgage payments and private mortgage insurance (PMI), which is an additional cost that protects the lender in case you default on the loan.

To save for a down payment, create a dedicated savings plan that includes regular contributions to a savings account. Look for areas in your budget where you can cut back on discretionary spending, such as dining out or entertainment, and redirect those funds toward your down payment goal. Additionally, consider setting up automatic transfers from your checking account to your savings account to ensure consistent progress.

Pre-Approval Process

Before you start house hunting, it's a good idea to get pre-approved for a mortgage. Pre-approval is a process in which a lender reviews your financial information, including your income, credit score, and debt, to determine how much they are willing to lend you. A pre-approval letter shows sellers that you're a serious buyer and gives you a clear idea of your budget.

To get pre-approved, you'll need to provide the lender with various documents, such as pay stubs, tax returns, bank statements, and information about your debts and assets. The lender will also perform a credit check to assess your creditworthiness. Once you're pre-approved, the lender will provide you with a pre-approval letter that outlines the loan amount you qualify for and the interest rate you're likely to receive.

Having a pre-approval letter in hand can give you a competitive edge in a hot real estate market, as it demonstrates to sellers that you're financially capable of purchasing their home. It also allows you to make a more informed decision when making an offer, as you'll know exactly how much you can afford to spend.

In summary, preparing to buy a home involves assessing your financial health, understanding your credit score, saving for a down payment, and getting pre-approved for a mortgage. By taking these steps, you'll be better equipped to navigate the homebuying process and achieve your goal of homeownership.

Chapter 3: Understanding Your Homebuying Needs

When it comes to buying a home, one size does not fit all. Every homebuyer has unique needs, preferences, and priorities that influence their decision-making process. Understanding what you're looking for in a home is a critical step in finding the perfect property that meets both your immediate needs and long-term goals. In this chapter, we'll explore how to define your homebuying needs, consider key factors like location, size, and style, and make informed decisions during your search.

Defining Your Must-Haves and Nice-to-Haves

Before you start looking at homes, it's important to clearly define your must-haves and nice-to-haves. Must-haves are the non-negotiable features that your new home must include, while nice-to-haves are features that would be a bonus but aren't essential.

To get started, sit down and make a list of the things that are most important to you in a home. This might include the number of bedrooms and bathrooms, whether the home has a garage, the size of the backyard, or the layout of the kitchen. These are the features you cannot compromise on.

Next, think about your nice-to-haves. These are features that would be great to have but aren't deal-breakers if they're missing. Maybe you'd love a home with a pool, but it's not a necessity. Or perhaps you'd like a walk-in closet, but you're willing to forgo it if the rest of the home meets your needs.

For example, consider Carlos and Maria, a young couple expecting their first child. They decided that a minimum of three bedrooms was a must-have, as they wanted a bedroom for themselves, a nursery for the baby, and a guest room for visiting family. Additionally, they both work from home, so a home office space was non-negotiable. However, they considered features like a finished basement or a large backyard as nice-to-haves—something they'd love but could live without if they found the right home otherwise.

Defining your must-haves and nice-to-haves will help you stay focused during your home search and avoid getting sidetracked by properties that don't meet your core needs. It will also make it easier for your REALPRO agent to understand what you're looking for and narrow down the list of potential homes.

Considering Location, Size, and Style

Location is one of the most critical factors in the homebuying process. The right location can enhance your quality of life, while the wrong one can lead to regrets. When considering location, think about proximity to work, schools, shopping centers, and recreational facilities. Also, consider the neighborhood's safety, future development plans, and overall vibe. For instance, if you value a quiet, family-friendly atmosphere, you might prioritize neighborhoods with low traffic, good schools, and plenty of parks.

Size is another important consideration. The size of the home should align with your current needs and future plans. If you're planning to grow your family, a home with extra bedrooms or a flexible layout might be ideal. On the other hand, if you're downsizing, a smaller, more manageable space may be more appealing. Consider not only the number of rooms but also the overall square footage and how the space is distributed.

Style is often a reflection of personal taste and lifestyle. Some people prefer the charm of a traditional colonial home, while others are drawn to the clean lines and open spaces of a modern, contemporary design. Think about what style resonates with you and how it aligns with your day-to-day living. For example, a single-story ranch might be perfect for someone who prefers a more accessible layout, while a multi-level home with a grand staircase might appeal to those who love architectural drama.

Take the example of Jian and Li, a couple in their late 30s with two young children. They prioritized finding a home in a neighborhood known for its excellent school district. Additionally, they wanted a home with enough space for their kids to play and grow, so they looked for properties with large backyards and extra rooms that could serve as playrooms or study areas. While they admired the sleek lines of contemporary homes, they ultimately chose a spacious, traditional two-story house with a large yard, located in a quiet, suburban area with top-rated schools.

Making Informed Decisions

Understanding your homebuying needs and how they align with your budget is crucial in making informed decisions. It's easy to get caught up in the excitement of finding the perfect home, but it's important to stay grounded in reality. Work closely with your REALPRO agent to evaluate each property's pros and cons, considering how well it meets your must-haves, nice-to-haves, and budget.

For example, during the search, you might come across a home that checks almost all your must-have boxes but lacks one or two nice-to-haves. In such cases, it's essential to weigh the trade-offs and determine whether the home's strengths outweigh its shortcomings. Your REALPRO agent can provide valuable insights into the local market, helping you understand whether you're getting good value for the price and whether it's worth compromising on certain features.

In summary, understanding your homebuying needs involves clearly defining your must-haves and nice-to-haves, carefully considering location, size, and style, and making informed decisions with the guidance of your REALPRO agent. By taking the time to assess what you truly need in a home, you'll be better equipped to find a property that not only meets your current needs but also supports your long-term goals.

Chapter 4: Finding the Right Real Estate Agent

Navigating the complexities of the homebuying process can be overwhelming, especially for first-time buyers. That's where a knowledgeable and experienced real estate agent comes in. The right agent can make all the difference in your homebuying journey, from helping you find the perfect property to negotiating the best deal. In this chapter, we'll explore why working with a REALPRO agent is advantageous, how to choose the right agent for your needs, and the role your agent plays throughout the process.

Why Work with a REALPRO Agent?

Choosing a real estate agent is one of the most important decisions you'll make during your homebuying journey. A REALPRO agent brings local expertise, market knowledge, and a commitment to exceptional service. Whether you're buying your first home or your fifth, a REALPRO agent can guide you through the process with confidence and ease.

One of the primary advantages of working with a REALPRO agent is their deep understanding of the local market. Real estate markets can vary significantly from one area to another, and having an agent who knows the nuances of your desired location is invaluable. For example, a REALPRO agent can provide insights into which neighborhoods are on the rise, where property values are likely to increase, and which areas might not be the best investment.

REALPRO agents are also skilled negotiators. When it comes time to make an offer, your agent will use their knowledge of the market and the property to help you craft a competitive offer that aligns with your budget and goals. They can also advise you on when it might be appropriate to ask for concessions, such as repairs or price reductions, and when it's best to make a strong, straightforward offer.

Moreover, a REALPRO agent is dedicated to your success. They'll take the time to understand your unique needs and preferences, and they'll work tirelessly to find properties that meet your criteria. Throughout the process, they'll keep you informed, answer your questions, and provide expert advice, ensuring that you feel confident and supported every step of the way.

How to Choose the Right Agent

Selecting the right real estate agent is a personal decision, and it's important to find someone you feel comfortable with and trust. Here are some key factors to consider when choosing an agent:

1. **Experience and Expertise**: Look for an agent with a proven track record of success in the type of property you're interested in. For example, if you're buying a single-family home, an agent with experience in that market segment will be more knowledgeable about pricing, competition, and potential pitfalls.
2. **Local Knowledge**: A good agent should have extensive knowledge of the local area, including neighborhoods, schools, amenities, and market trends. Ask potential agents about their experience in the specific areas you're considering.

3. **Communication Style**: Effective communication is key to a successful partnership with your agent. During your initial meetings, pay attention to how well the agent listens to your needs, answers your questions, and explains the process. You should feel comfortable asking questions and expressing concerns.
4. **References and Reviews**: Don't hesitate to ask for references from past clients or to read online reviews. This can provide valuable insight into the agent's professionalism, reliability, and ability to deliver results.
5. **Availability**: Make sure the agent is available when you need them, especially if you're working with a tight timeline. Ask about their availability for showings, meetings, and communications, and ensure they're able to accommodate your schedule.

Consider the experience of Miguel and Sofia, who were looking for their first home. They interviewed several agents but ultimately chose a REALPRO agent who not only had extensive experience in the local market but also took the time to understand their unique needs as first-time buyers. The agent's patience, clear communication, and willingness to answer all their questions made the process much less stressful for the couple.

The Role of a REALPRO Agent

A REALPRO agent plays a crucial role throughout the homebuying process, serving as your advocate, advisor, and guide. Here's what you can expect from your agent at each stage of the journey:

1. **Initial Consultation**: Your agent will start by getting to know you—your needs, preferences, budget, and goals. They'll ask about your must-haves and nice-to-haves, your preferred location, and any concerns you might have. This consultation sets the foundation for your home search.
2. **Property Search**: Using their local market knowledge and access to listings, your agent will identify properties that meet your criteria. They'll arrange showings, accompany you to viewings, and provide feedback on each property's potential.
3. **Market Analysis**: Your agent will provide you with a comparative market analysis (CMA) to help you understand how the property you're interested in compares to similar homes in the area. This analysis is crucial for making an informed offer.
4. **Making an Offer**: When you're ready to make an offer, your agent will help you determine a fair and competitive price based on market conditions, the property's value, and your budget. They'll also advise you on contingencies, such as inspections and financing, to include in your offer.
5. **Negotiations**: If the seller makes a counteroffer or if issues arise during the inspection, your agent will handle negotiations on your behalf. Their goal is to secure the best possible terms for you while ensuring the deal stays on track.
6. **Closing**: As closing day approaches, your agent will guide you through the final steps, including reviewing documents, attending the final walkthrough, and coordinating with your lender and attorney. They'll ensure

that everything is in order so you can close with confidence.

In summary, finding the right real estate agent is a critical step in the homebuying process. A REALPRO agent offers local expertise, market knowledge, and a commitment to your success, making them an invaluable partner on your journey to homeownership. By choosing the right agent, you can navigate the complexities of the market with confidence and achieve your homebuying goals.

Buying A Home?
Visit www.realprointernational.com
scan below

Or call
1-855-310-HOME

Chapter 5: Navigating the Real Estate Market

The real estate market can be complex and ever-changing, with factors such as economic conditions, interest rates, and local trends all playing a role in determining property values and availability. As a homebuyer, understanding the market is essential for making informed decisions and getting the best possible deal on your new home. In this chapter, we'll explore how to navigate the real estate market, including understanding market conditions, researching homes and neighborhoods, and making the most of property viewings.

Understanding Market Conditions

The real estate market can be classified into two main types: a buyer's market and a seller's market. Knowing which type of market you're in is crucial for shaping your buying strategy.

In a **buyer's market**, there are more homes for sale than there are buyers. This creates favorable conditions for buyers, as sellers may be more willing to negotiate on price and terms to secure a sale. In a buyer's market, you might find that homes stay on the market longer, and you have more options to choose from. This can give you the leverage to negotiate a lower price or ask for additional concessions, such as the seller covering closing costs or making repairs.

Conversely, in a **seller's market**, there are more buyers than there are homes for sale. This often leads to increased competition among buyers, with multiple offers on desirable properties. In a seller's market, prices tend to rise, and buyers may need to act quickly and make strong offers to secure a home. It's not uncommon in a seller's market to see homes selling above the asking price, especially if they're in high-demand areas.

To illustrate, imagine Maria and Juan, who were searching for a home during a seller's market. They found a property they loved but quickly realized they weren't the only ones interested. With several other offers on the table, their REALPRO agent advised them to make a competitive offer slightly above the asking price and to consider waiving certain contingencies to strengthen their bid. While this approach carried some risk, it ultimately helped them secure the home in a highly competitive market.

Understanding whether you're in a buyer's or seller's market will help you set realistic expectations and develop an appropriate strategy for making an offer. Your REALPRO agent can provide valuable insights into current market conditions and advise you on the best approach based on your specific situation.

How to Research Homes and Neighborhoods

Before you start visiting properties, it's important to do your homework. Researching homes and neighborhoods will give you a better understanding of what's available, what fits your budget, and what areas align with your lifestyle.

Start by browsing listings on the REALPRO agents' website, where you can search for homes based on criteria such as price, location, size, and features. Pay attention to the property descriptions, photos, and virtual tours, which can give you a good sense of the home's layout, condition, and amenities.

In addition to researching individual properties, take the time to learn about the neighborhoods you're considering. Look into factors such as:

- **School Districts**: If you have children or plan to in the future, the quality of the local school district can be a major consideration. Research school ratings, test scores, and reviews to understand the educational opportunities available.
- **Crime Rates**: Safety is a top priority for most homebuyers. Check local crime statistics to get a sense of the neighborhood's safety, and consider visiting the area at different times of the day to observe the environment.
- **Amenities and Services**: Consider the proximity of grocery stores, restaurants, parks, public transportation, and other amenities that are important to you. A neighborhood with easy access to these services can enhance your quality of life and convenience.
- **Future Development**: Research any planned developments in the area, such as new roads, commercial projects, or housing developments. While some developments can increase property values, others may lead to increased traffic or noise.

Take the example of Aisha, who was looking for a home in a family-friendly neighborhood. She used online tools to research school districts and crime rates, narrowing down her options to a few neighborhoods that met her criteria. With her REALPRO agent's help, she then visited each neighborhood to get a feel for the community, talk to local residents, and assess the amenities. This thorough research helped her make an informed decision and find a home in a neighborhood that was perfect for her family.

Visiting Open Houses and Private Showings

Once you've done your research, it's time to start visiting properties. Whether you're attending an open house or scheduling a private showing, these visits are an opportunity to see the home in person, ask questions, and assess whether it meets your needs.

During property visits, pay close attention to both the positives and potential drawbacks. Here are some key things to look for:

- **Structural Integrity**: Examine the home's foundation, roof, and exterior for any signs of damage or wear. Inside, look for cracks in the walls, water stains, or uneven floors, which could indicate underlying issues.
- **Layout and Flow**: Consider how the home's layout fits your lifestyle. Does the kitchen flow well into the dining and living areas? Are the bedrooms and bathrooms conveniently located? Think about how the space will work for your daily routines.
- **Natural Light**: Take note of the natural light in each room. A home with plenty of windows and good exposure can feel more inviting and reduce the need for artificial lighting.
- **Storage Space**: Check for adequate storage, including closets, cabinets, and attic or basement space. Sufficient storage is essential for keeping your home organized and clutter-free.

- **Neighborhood Vibe**: As you walk through the neighborhood, pay attention to the condition of other homes, the presence of parks or green spaces, and the overall atmosphere. Does it feel welcoming and well-maintained?

During the visit, don't hesitate to ask your REALPRO agent questions about the property, such as the age of major systems (roof, HVAC, plumbing), recent updates, and any known issues. Your agent can also provide insights into the home's pricing and how it compares to similar properties in the area.

For example, during a private showing, David and Emily, a young couple, noticed some signs of wear on the roof and a few cracks in the basement walls. They brought their concerns to their REALPRO agent, who arranged for a home inspection to assess the extent of the issues. The inspection revealed that the roof would need to be replaced within a few years, which gave them leverage to negotiate a lower purchase price.

Chapter 6: Making an Offer

Once you've found the right home, the next step is to make an offer. This is where your real estate agent's expertise and negotiation skills come into play. Crafting a compelling offer requires a balance of strategy, timing, and understanding of the current market conditions. In this chapter, we'll discuss how to make a strong offer, the role of contingencies, and how your REALPRO agent can help you secure the best possible deal.

Understanding Offer Strategies

The strategy behind your offer will depend on several factors, including the current market conditions, the home's listing price, and how long the property has been on the market. In a competitive seller's market, where multiple buyers are vying for the same property, you may need to act quickly and make a strong offer to stand out. On the other hand, in a buyer's market, where there are more homes for sale than buyers, you may have more room to negotiate.

Before making an offer, your REALPRO agent will conduct a comparative market analysis (CMA) to determine the fair market value of the property. This analysis compares the home you're interested in with similar properties that have recently sold in the area. The CMA will help you understand whether the listing price is reasonable and what a competitive offer would be.

Let's consider an example. Isabel and Roberto were looking at a home listed for $350,000. Their REALPRO agent conducted a CMA and found that similar homes in the neighborhood had recently sold for between $340,000 and $360,000. Given the market conditions and the home's features, the agent recommended an offer of $345,000, which was competitive yet slightly below the asking price. Isabel and Roberto trusted their agent's expertise, made the offer, and ultimately secured the home at a price they were comfortable with.

Writing a Strong Offer

A strong offer is more than just a dollar amount—it's a package that includes the price, terms, and contingencies. Here are some key components to consider when crafting your offer:

1. **Purchase Price**: The purchase price is the most critical element of your offer. While it's tempting to make a low offer to save money, a bid that's too low can be rejected outright, especially in a competitive market. Your REALPRO agent will help you determine a fair and competitive price based on the CMA and market conditions.
2. **Earnest Money Deposit**: The earnest money deposit is a sum of money you put down as a show of good faith when making an offer. It demonstrates to the seller that you're serious about purchasing the home. Typically, earnest money amounts to 1% to 3% of the purchase price, although it can vary depending on the market. This deposit is held in escrow and applied to your down payment or closing costs if the offer is accepted.
3. **Contingencies**: Contingencies are conditions that must be met for the sale to proceed. Common contingencies include financing, home inspection, and appraisal. For

example, a financing contingency allows you to back out of the deal if you're unable to secure a mortgage. An inspection contingency gives you the right to have the home inspected and request repairs or renegotiate the price based on the findings. Including contingencies in your offer protects you from unforeseen issues, but be mindful that too many contingencies can weaken your offer in a competitive market.

4. **Closing Timeline**: The closing timeline refers to the period between the offer acceptance and the closing date when ownership is officially transferred. A typical closing timeline ranges from 30 to 45 days, but this can vary based on the buyer's financing and the seller's needs. If the seller is looking to close quickly, offering a shorter timeline can make your offer more attractive.

5. **Personal Letter**: In some cases, buyers include a personal letter with their offer to establish an emotional connection with the seller. While this isn't always necessary, it can be a helpful touch, especially if multiple offers are on the table. The letter should express your appreciation for the home and explain why it's the perfect fit for you and your family.

How Your REALPRO Agent Assists

Your REALPRO agent plays a vital role in crafting and submitting your offer. They'll provide guidance on pricing, help you decide which contingencies to include, and ensure that your offer is presented in the best possible light. Once the offer is submitted, your agent will handle negotiations with the seller's agent, working to secure favorable terms on your behalf.

For instance, when Marcus and Lila found their dream home, they were concerned about the potential for multiple offers. Their REALPRO agent advised them to make an offer slightly above the asking price and to waive the inspection contingency, as they were confident in the home's condition. This strategic move helped their offer stand out, and the sellers accepted it over others that were less flexible.

In summary, making an offer is a critical step in the homebuying process that requires careful consideration and strategy. By working closely with your REALPRO agent, you can craft a strong offer that reflects your budget, protects your interests, and increases your chances of securing the home you love.

Chapter 7: The Home Inspection

The home inspection is one of the most critical steps in the homebuying process. It's an opportunity for you to assess the condition of the property you're about to purchase and identify any potential issues that could affect its value or livability. A thorough inspection can save you from unexpected repairs and expenses down the road, giving you peace of mind and leverage in negotiations. In this chapter, we'll explore why inspections matter, common issues found during inspections, and how to negotiate repairs or price adjustments based on the findings.

Why Inspections Matter

Buying a home is a significant investment, and the last thing you want is to discover major problems after you've closed the deal. A home inspection provides an in-depth evaluation of the property's condition, covering everything from the foundation to the roof. The goal is to uncover any hidden issues that may not be visible during a regular walkthrough, such as structural damage, electrical problems, or plumbing leaks.

For example, let's say you're considering purchasing a charming older home that has recently been renovated. While the home's updated kitchen and bathrooms may look beautiful, an inspection could reveal underlying issues, such as outdated wiring, a leaky roof, or a faulty HVAC system. Without an inspection, these problems might not become apparent until after you've moved in, leading to costly repairs that could have been avoided.

An inspection also provides you with a detailed report that outlines the condition of the home and any repairs or maintenance that may be needed. This report is a valuable tool for making an informed decision about whether to proceed with the purchase, request repairs, or negotiate a lower price. In some cases, the inspection may reveal issues so severe that you decide to walk away from the deal altogether, saving you from a bad investment.

Common Issues Found in Inspections

Home inspections can uncover a wide range of issues, some of which are minor and easily fixable, while others may require significant repairs. Here are some common problems that inspectors often find:

1. **Roof Damage**: Roofs are one of the most important components of a home, protecting it from the elements. Inspectors often find issues such as missing or damaged shingles, leaks, and poor ventilation. Depending on the severity, roof repairs can be costly, so it's essential to address any problems before closing.
2. **Foundation Issues**: The foundation is critical to the structural integrity of the home. Inspectors look for signs of foundation problems, such as cracks in the walls, uneven floors, or doors and windows that don't close properly. Foundation repairs can be expensive and complex, making this a key area of concern during an inspection.
3. **Plumbing Problems**: Inspectors check the home's plumbing system for leaks, water pressure issues, and

outdated materials like lead pipes. Leaks can lead to water damage and mold growth, while outdated plumbing may need to be replaced to ensure safe water quality.
4. **Electrical Issues**: Outdated or faulty electrical systems pose a safety hazard and can lead to fires. Inspectors examine the home's wiring, electrical panels, and outlets to ensure they meet current safety standards. Common issues include outdated knob-and-tube wiring, overloaded circuits, and insufficient grounding.
5. **HVAC System**: The heating, ventilation, and air conditioning (HVAC) system is responsible for maintaining a comfortable indoor environment. Inspectors check the system's age, condition, and functionality, looking for signs of wear and tear or inefficiency. Replacing an HVAC system can be expensive, so it's important to know if the system is near the end of its lifespan.
6. **Water Damage and Mold**: Inspectors look for signs of water damage, such as stains on walls or ceilings, musty odors, or visible mold growth. Water damage can lead to structural issues and health concerns, especially if mold is present. Addressing water damage and mold remediation can be costly, so these issues should be taken seriously.
7. **Pest Infestations**: Inspectors check for signs of pest infestations, such as termites, rodents, or carpenter ants. Pests can cause significant damage to a home's structure and require professional extermination.

Negotiating Repairs or Price Adjustments

Once the inspection is complete, you'll receive a detailed report outlining the findings. If the inspection uncovers issues that need to be addressed, you have several options for moving forward:

1. **Request Repairs**: You can ask the seller to make the necessary repairs before closing. This is a common approach, especially for issues that are essential to the home's safety and functionality. For example, if the inspection reveals that the roof needs repairs, you can request that the seller fix it before you proceed with the purchase.
2. **Negotiate a Price Reduction**: If the seller is unwilling or unable to make the repairs, you can negotiate a reduction in the purchase price to account for the cost of the repairs. This option allows you to take care of the repairs after closing, giving you control over the quality of the work.
3. **Ask for a Repair Credit**: Instead of asking the seller to make repairs, you can request a credit at closing to cover the cost of the repairs. This option is often preferred when buyers want to choose their own contractors or when the repairs are not urgent.
4. **Walk Away**: In some cases, the inspection may reveal issues that are too costly or complex to address. If the problems are significant and the seller is unwilling to negotiate, you may decide to walk away from the deal. This is why including an inspection contingency in your offer is so important—it gives you the option to back out of the deal without losing your earnest money.

Consider the experience of Javier and Leticia, who were in the process of buying a home when their inspection revealed significant foundation issues. The estimated cost of repairs was well beyond their budget, and the seller was unwilling to negotiate. With the advice of their REALPRO agent, they decided to walk away from the deal and continue their search for a home that met their needs without the added risk and expense.

In summary, a home inspection is a crucial step in the homebuying process that provides you with a clear understanding of the property's condition. By identifying potential issues and using the inspection report to negotiate repairs or price adjustments, you can protect your investment and ensure that your new home is a safe and sound purchase.

Chapter 8: Securing a Mortgage

Securing a mortgage is a pivotal part of the homebuying process, as it determines how much you can afford to spend on a home and the terms of your loan. Understanding the various mortgage options, choosing the right lender, and locking in a favorable interest rate are all crucial steps in financing your home purchase. In this chapter, we'll explore the different types of mortgages available, how to choose the right lender, and the role your REALPRO agent plays in helping you secure the best possible loan.

Understanding Mortgage Options

There are several types of mortgages available, each with its own set of terms, benefits, and eligibility requirements. The most common types of mortgages include fixed-rate mortgages, adjustable-rate mortgages (ARMs), and government-backed loans such as FHA, VA, and USDA loans. Understanding the differences between these options is key to choosing the one that best suits your financial situation and long-term goals.

1. **Fixed-Rate Mortgages**: A fixed-rate mortgage is the most straightforward type of home loan, offering a stable interest rate that remains unchanged throughout the life of the loan. This predictability makes it an attractive option for many homebuyers, as your monthly mortgage payments will remain consistent, regardless of fluctuations in interest rates. Fixed-rate mortgages are typically available in 15-, 20-, or 30-year terms, with the 30-year fixed-rate mortgage being the most popular

choice. While a 30-year mortgage offers lower monthly payments, a 15-year mortgage allows you to pay off your loan faster and save on interest over the life of the loan.

2. **Adjustable-Rate Mortgages (ARMs)**: An adjustable-rate mortgage offers an initial period of fixed interest, usually lower than that of a fixed-rate mortgage, followed by periodic adjustments based on market conditions. For example, a 5/1 ARM has a fixed interest rate for the first five years, after which the rate adjusts annually based on the lender's benchmark rate. While ARMs can offer lower initial payments, they come with the risk of increased payments if interest rates rise. ARMs may be a good option for buyers who plan to sell or refinance before the adjustable period begins.

3. **FHA Loans**: Backed by the Federal Housing Administration, FHA loans are designed to help first-time homebuyers or those with less-than-perfect credit qualify for a mortgage. FHA loans require a lower down payment (as little as 3.5%) and have more lenient credit requirements than conventional loans. However, borrowers are required to pay mortgage insurance premiums (MIP), which increases the overall cost of the loan.

4. **VA Loans**: VA loans are available to veterans, active-duty service members, and eligible surviving spouses, offering a range of benefits, including no down payment, no mortgage insurance, and competitive interest rates. VA loans are backed by the U.S. Department of Veterans Affairs and are designed to make homeownership more accessible for those who have served in the military.

5. **USDA Loans**: The U.S. Department of Agriculture offers USDA loans to help low- to moderate-income buyers purchase homes in eligible rural and suburban areas. USDA loans require no down payment and offer competitive interest rates, making them an attractive option for buyers in qualifying areas. However, there are income limits and property eligibility requirements to qualify for a USDA loan.

Choosing the Right Lender

Once you've decided on the type of mortgage that's right for you, the next step is to choose a lender. Shopping around for a mortgage lender can help you secure the best interest rate and terms, potentially saving you thousands of dollars over the life of your loan. Here are some key factors to consider when choosing a lender:

1. **Interest Rates**: The interest rate is one of the most important factors to consider when choosing a mortgage lender. Even a small difference in interest rates can have a significant impact on your monthly payments and the total cost of your loan. Compare rates from multiple lenders to ensure you're getting the best deal.
2. **Fees and Closing Costs**: In addition to interest rates, lenders may charge various fees, including origination fees, application fees, and closing costs. These fees can add up, so it's important to understand the total cost of the loan and compare the fees charged by different lenders.

3. **Loan Terms**: Consider the loan terms offered by each lender, including the length of the loan, whether the rate is fixed or adjustable, and any prepayment penalties. Make sure the terms align with your financial goals and timeline.
4. **Customer Service**: A lender's reputation for customer service is also an important consideration. You want a lender who is responsive, transparent, and willing to answer your questions throughout the mortgage process. Reading online reviews and asking for recommendations from friends or your REALPRO agent can help you find a lender with a strong track record.
5. **Pre-Approval Process**: Some lenders offer a quick and easy pre-approval process, which can give you an edge when making an offer on a home. Getting pre-approved by a reputable lender shows sellers that you're a serious buyer and can close the deal quickly.

Consider the experience of Diego and Ana, who were shopping for their first home. They initially went with a lender recommended by a friend but quickly realized that the interest rate and fees were higher than they expected. With the help of their REALPRO agent, they shopped around and found another lender who offered a lower interest rate and waived some of the fees, saving them thousands of dollars over the life of their loan.

How Interest Rates Affect Your Mortgage

Interest rates play a crucial role in determining the affordability of your mortgage. Even a slight change in interest rates can have a significant impact on your monthly payments and the total amount you'll pay over the life of the loan. Here's how it works:

- **Monthly Payments**: The interest rate directly affects your monthly mortgage payment. For example, on a $300,000 loan with a 30-year term, a 4% interest rate would result in a monthly payment of approximately $1,432 (excluding taxes and insurance). If the interest rate were to increase to 5%, the monthly payment would rise to approximately $1,610—an increase of $178 per month, or over $64,000 over the life of the loan.
- **Total Interest Paid**: Over the life of the loan, the interest rate determines how much you'll pay in interest. Using the same example, with a 4% interest rate, you would pay approximately $215,000 in interest over 30 years. With a 5% interest rate, you would pay approximately $279,000 in interest—an increase of $64,000.
- **Loan-to-Value Ratio (LTV)**: The interest rate can also impact your loan-to-value ratio, which is the ratio of your loan amount to the appraised value of the home. A lower interest rate may allow you to afford a higher loan amount while keeping your monthly payments within your budget, potentially increasing your LTV ratio.

Given the importance of interest rates, it's essential to lock in a favorable rate when you find one that fits your budget. Your REALPRO agent can help you monitor interest rates and advise you on the best time to lock in your rate, ensuring you get the best possible terms for your mortgage.

The Role of Your Agent in Mortgage Negotiations

Your REALPRO agent is more than just a guide through the homebuying process—they're also an advocate in securing the best financing options for your purchase. Here's how your agent can assist in the mortgage process:

- **Lender Recommendations**: Your REALPRO agent can recommend reputable lenders who offer competitive rates and excellent customer service. They can also help you compare different lenders and loan options to find the best fit for your needs.
- **Rate Lock Guidance**: Interest rates can fluctuate daily, and your agent can provide guidance on when to lock in your rate. By staying informed about market trends, your agent can help you secure a favorable rate at the right time.
- **Negotiating Closing Costs**: In some cases, your REALPRO agent can help negotiate with the seller to cover some or all of the closing costs. This can reduce your out-of-pocket expenses and make the purchase more affordable.
- **Coordinating with the Lender**: Throughout the process, your agent will work closely with your lender to ensure that everything is on track for a smooth closing. They'll coordinate the appraisal, inspection, and other steps to keep the process moving forward.

Chapter 9: The Appraisal Process

The appraisal process is a crucial step in the homebuying journey, as it determines the market value of the property you're purchasing. This value is used by lenders to ensure that they're not lending more than the property is worth, which protects both the lender and the buyer from overpaying. In this chapter, we'll explore what to expect during an appraisal, how appraisals affect your loan, and how to handle situations where the appraisal comes in lower than expected.

What to Expect During an Appraisal

An appraisal is an unbiased, professional assessment of a property's market value conducted by a licensed appraiser. The appraiser's job is to determine the fair market value of the home based on various factors, including its condition, location, and comparable sales (often referred to as "comps") in the area.

Here's what typically happens during the appraisal process:

1. **Property Inspection**: The appraiser will visit the property to conduct a thorough inspection. They'll examine both the interior and exterior of the home, noting its size, condition, layout, and any improvements or upgrades that have been made. The appraiser will also assess the overall quality of the construction and look for any signs of damage or deferred maintenance.
2. **Comparable Sales Analysis**: After the inspection, the appraiser will research recent sales of similar properties in the area. These comps help the appraiser determine how the subject property compares to other homes in

terms of size, condition, location, and features. The sales prices of these comps are used to help establish the market value of the property.
3. **Final Report**: The appraiser will compile their findings into a detailed report, which includes the appraised value of the property, an explanation of how the value was determined, and a description of the property and the comps used. This report is then submitted to the lender, who will use it to determine the maximum loan amount they're willing to provide.

The appraisal typically takes a few days to complete, and the cost is usually covered by the buyer as part of the closing costs. It's important to note that the appraiser works for the lender, not the buyer, and their primary responsibility is to ensure that the lender is making a sound investment.

How Appraisals Affect Your Loan

The appraisal has a direct impact on your mortgage, as lenders use the appraised value to determine the loan-to-value (LTV) ratio. The LTV ratio is the percentage of the loan amount relative to the appraised value of the property. For example, if you're purchasing a home for $300,000 and the appraisal comes in at $300,000, and you're putting down 20%, your LTV ratio would be 80% (a $240,000 loan on a $300,000 home).

If the appraisal comes in at or above the purchase price, the loan process typically proceeds as planned. However, if the appraisal comes in lower than the purchase price, it can create challenges for both the buyer and the lender. Here's why:

- **Loan Amount**: Lenders base the loan amount on the appraised value, not the purchase price. If the appraisal comes in lower than expected, the lender may reduce the amount they're willing to lend. For example, if you agreed to purchase a home for $300,000 but the appraisal comes in at $280,000, the lender will base the loan on the $280,000 value. If you're putting down 20%, this would result in a loan amount of $224,000, leaving you to cover the difference.
- **Down Payment**: A lower appraisal can also affect your down payment. Using the same example, if the appraisal comes in at $280,000 and you're putting down 20%, you would need to increase your down payment to cover the gap between the appraised value and the purchase price. This could mean coming up with an additional $20,000 out of pocket.
- **Private Mortgage Insurance (PMI)**: If the lower appraisal results in an LTV ratio higher than 80%, you may be required to pay PMI, which increases your monthly mortgage payment. PMI protects the lender in case you default on the loan.

Dealing with Low Appraisals

If the appraisal comes in lower than expected, there are several options for moving forward:

1. **Renegotiate the Price**: One of the most common solutions is to renegotiate the purchase price with the seller. If the appraisal comes in lower than the agreed-upon price, the seller may agree to lower the price to match the appraised

value. This can be a win-win situation, as it allows the sale to proceed while ensuring that you're not overpaying for the property.
2. **Increase Your Down Payment**: If the seller is unwilling to lower the price, you can choose to increase your down payment to cover the difference between the appraised value and the purchase price. This option allows you to proceed with the purchase without affecting the loan amount, but it requires you to come up with additional funds.
3. **Request a Reappraisal**: In some cases, you may have the option to request a reappraisal or a second opinion if you believe the initial appraisal was inaccurate or flawed. This is more likely to be successful if you can provide additional comps or evidence that the initial appraisal missed key factors affecting the property's value.
4. **Walk Away**: If the appraisal comes in significantly lower than the purchase price and you're unable to negotiate a solution, you may decide to walk away from the deal. This is why it's important to include an appraisal contingency in your offer, which allows you to back out of the contract without losing your earnest money if the appraisal comes in low.

Consider the experience of Aaliyah and Marcus, who were purchasing their first home. They agreed to a purchase price of $350,000, but the appraisal came in at $330,000. Their lender was only willing to provide a loan based on the $330,000 value, which meant they needed to cover the $20,000 difference out of pocket. After discussing their options with their REALPRO agent, they decided to renegotiate the price with the seller, who ultimately agreed to lower the price to $335,000. Aaliyah and Marcus increased their down payment slightly and were able to move forward with the purchase.

In summary, the appraisal process is a critical step that determines the market value of the property you're purchasing. Understanding how appraisals work and how they affect your mortgage can help you navigate this step with confidence. If the appraisal comes in lower than expected, there are several options for addressing the situation, including renegotiating the price, increasing your down payment, or requesting a reappraisal. By working closely with your REALPRO agent and lender, you can find a solution that works for your budget and ensures a successful home purchase.

Chapter 10: Preparing for Closing

As you approach the final stages of the homebuying process, preparing for closing is crucial to ensuring a smooth and successful transaction. Closing is the moment when ownership of the property is officially transferred from the seller to the buyer, and all financial and legal matters are settled. In this chapter, we'll explore what happens before closing, how to review the closing disclosure, and the steps involved in the final walkthrough to make sure everything is in order.

What Happens Before Closing?

The period between signing the purchase agreement and the closing date is often filled with anticipation and a flurry of activity. During this time, several important steps must be completed to ensure that the closing goes off without a hitch.

1. **Finalizing the Loan**: One of the key tasks before closing is finalizing your mortgage. Your lender will work with you to lock in your interest rate, review the terms of the loan, and ensure that all required documentation is in place. This includes providing proof of homeowners insurance, which is necessary to protect both you and the lender. The lender will also conduct a final credit check and verify your employment status to confirm that nothing has changed since your initial loan application.
2. **Title Search and Insurance**: A title search is conducted to verify that the seller has clear ownership of the property and that there are no outstanding liens, claims, or legal issues that could affect the transfer of ownership. The title

company will issue a title insurance policy to protect you and the lender from any future claims against the property. Title insurance is a one-time cost paid at closing and is a crucial safeguard against potential legal disputes.
3. **Homeowners Insurance**: Before closing, you'll need to secure homeowners insurance, which is required by most lenders. Homeowners insurance covers the structure of the home and your personal belongings in the event of damage or loss due to fire, theft, or other covered perils. It's important to compare policies from different insurance providers to find the best coverage at the most affordable rate.
4. **Appraisal and Inspection Review**: By this point, the appraisal and home inspection should already be completed. If any issues were found during the inspection, you'll need to confirm that the seller has made the necessary repairs or that you've agreed on any price adjustments. Your REALPRO agent will help you review the appraisal and inspection reports to ensure that everything is in order.
5. **Reviewing the Closing Disclosure**: A few days before closing, your lender will provide you with the closing disclosure, a document that outlines the final terms of your loan, including the interest rate, monthly payments, and closing costs. It's essential to review this document carefully and compare it to the loan estimate you received earlier in the process to ensure that there are no unexpected changes.

Reviewing the Closing Disclosure

The closing disclosure is one of the most important documents you'll receive during the homebuying process. It provides a detailed summary of your loan and all the costs associated with closing, giving you a clear picture of what you'll need to pay on closing day.

Here's what to look for when reviewing the closing disclosure:

1. **Loan Terms**: The first section of the closing disclosure outlines the loan terms, including the loan amount, interest rate, and monthly principal and interest payment. Verify that these terms match the terms you agreed to with your lender.
2. **Projected Payments**: This section breaks down your monthly mortgage payment, including principal, interest, property taxes, homeowners insurance, and any private mortgage insurance (PMI) if applicable. It also shows how your payments may change over time, especially if you have an adjustable-rate mortgage.
3. **Closing Costs**: The closing disclosure provides a detailed breakdown of all closing costs, including lender fees, title insurance, appraisal fees, and other charges. Compare these costs to the loan estimate you received earlier to ensure they are in line with your expectations.
4. **Cash to Close**: This section shows the total amount of money you'll need to bring to closing, including your down payment, closing costs, and any credits or adjustments. Make sure you have sufficient funds in your account to

cover this amount, as you'll need to pay it by certified check or wire transfer on closing day.

5. **Escrow Account**: If your lender requires an escrow account to cover property taxes and insurance, the closing disclosure will outline the initial escrow payment required at closing. This payment ensures that there are sufficient funds in the account to cover these expenses when they come due.

If you notice any discrepancies or have questions about the closing disclosure, contact your lender and REALPRO agent immediately. It's important to address any issues before closing day to avoid delays or complications.

Final Walkthrough Checklist

The final walkthrough is your last opportunity to inspect the property before closing. It typically takes place 24 to 48 hours before the closing date and allows you to confirm that the property is in the condition agreed upon in the purchase contract.

During the final walkthrough, you'll want to ensure that:

1. **Repairs Have Been Completed**: If the seller agreed to make any repairs based on the home inspection, verify that these repairs have been completed to your satisfaction. Bring a copy of the inspection report and the repair agreement to the walkthrough to check off each item.
2. **Appliances Are in Working Order**: Test all major appliances, including the stove, refrigerator, dishwasher,

washer, and dryer, to ensure they are functioning properly. If any appliances were included in the sale, confirm that they are still in the home and in good condition.
3. **No New Damage**: Check for any new damage to the property that may have occurred since the inspection. This includes looking for water leaks, cracked windows, or any other issues that were not present during previous visits.
4. **All Agreed-Upon Items Are Present**: Ensure that any fixtures, furniture, or other items that were included in the sale are still in the home. This might include things like light fixtures, window treatments, or outdoor furniture.
5. **Utilities Are Functioning**: Test the heating, air conditioning, plumbing, and electrical systems to make sure everything is in working order. Turn on all the lights, faucets, and flush toilets to check for any issues.
6. **House Is Clean**: While the property doesn't need to be spotless, it should be reasonably clean and free of the seller's belongings. If the home is still cluttered with the seller's items or there's excessive dirt or debris, address this with your REALPRO agent.

Consider the experience of Elena and Victor, who were excited to move into their new home. During the final walkthrough, they discovered that the seller had removed several light fixtures that were supposed to be included in the sale. Their REALPRO agent immediately contacted the seller's agent, and the issue was resolved before closing, with the seller agreeing to reinstall the fixtures.

After the final walkthrough, if everything is in order, you're ready to proceed to closing. If any issues arise during the walkthrough, your REALPRO agent will work quickly to address them and ensure that they are resolved before closing day.

In summary, preparing for closing involves finalizing your loan, reviewing the closing disclosure, and conducting a final walkthrough of the property. By carefully following these steps and working closely with your REALPRO agent, you can ensure that closing day goes smoothly and that you're fully prepared to take ownership of your new home.

Buying A Home?
Visit www.realprointernational.com
scan below

Or call
1-855-310-HOME

Chapter 11: Closing Day

Closing day is the culmination of your homebuying journey—an exciting moment when ownership of the property is officially transferred to you. However, it's also a day filled with important tasks, paperwork, and financial transactions. Understanding what to expect on closing day and how to prepare can help ensure that everything goes smoothly and that you walk away with the keys to your new home. In this chapter, we'll explore the closing process, the documents you'll sign, and the costs involved in closing.

Understanding Closing Costs

Closing costs are the fees and expenses associated with finalizing your mortgage and transferring ownership of the property. These costs typically range from 2% to 5% of the home's purchase price and are paid at closing. It's important to be aware of these costs in advance so that you're fully prepared to cover them on closing day.

Here's a breakdown of common closing costs:

1. **Loan Origination Fee**: This fee is charged by the lender for processing your mortgage application. It typically ranges from 0.5% to 1% of the loan amount.
2. **Appraisal Fee**: The appraisal fee covers the cost of having the property appraised to determine its market value. This fee is usually between $300 and $500.
3. **Title Insurance**: Title insurance protects you and the lender from any legal disputes or claims against the property's title. The cost of title insurance varies based on

the property's value and the location but typically ranges from $500 to $1,500.
4. **Attorney Fees**: In some states, it's customary to have an attorney present at closing to review the documents and ensure that everything is in order. Attorney fees can vary but are generally around $500 to $1,000.
5. **Recording Fees**: These fees are charged by the local government to record the sale of the property and the mortgage in public records. Recording fees typically range from $100 to $200.
6. **Prepaid Expenses**: Prepaid expenses include property taxes, homeowners insurance, and interest that must be paid in advance. These amounts are usually collected at closing and placed in an escrow account to cover future payments.
7. **Private Mortgage Insurance (PMI)**: If your down payment is less than 20%, you may be required to pay PMI, which protects the lender in case you default on the loan. The cost of PMI varies but is usually between 0.3% and 1.5% of the original loan amount annually.
8. **Homeowners Association (HOA) Fees**: If the property is part of a homeowners association, you may need to pay prorated HOA fees at closing. These fees cover the cost of maintaining common areas and amenities.

Your lender will provide you with a final breakdown of all closing costs in the closing disclosure, which you should review carefully before closing day. Make sure you have sufficient funds to cover these costs, as they will need to be paid by certified check or wire transfer at closing.

The Documents You'll Sign

Closing day involves signing a significant amount of paperwork, much of which is related to your mortgage and the transfer of ownership. Here are some of the key documents you'll be signing:

1. **Promissory Note**: The promissory note is your promise to repay the mortgage loan according to the agreed-upon terms. It includes details such as the loan amount, interest rate, payment schedule, and the consequences of default.
2. **Deed of Trust or Mortgage**: This document secures the loan by placing a lien on the property. It gives the lender the right to foreclose on the property if you fail to repay the loan. The deed of trust or mortgage is recorded in public records as proof that the lender has a financial interest in the property.
3. **Closing Disclosure**: The closing disclosure provides a detailed summary of the loan terms, closing costs, and the total amount you'll need to pay at closing. You'll sign this document to confirm that you've reviewed and agreed to the terms.
4. **Deed**: The deed is the legal document that transfers ownership of the property from the seller to the buyer. It includes the names of the buyer and seller, a description of the property, and the signatures of both parties. Once signed, the deed is recorded in public records, officially making you the new owner.
5. **Affidavits and Declarations**: You may be required to sign various affidavits and declarations, such as an affidavit of title, which confirms that the seller has the legal right to

transfer ownership of the property, and a declaration of homestead, which may provide you with certain legal protections as a homeowner.
6. **Loan Application**: You'll also sign a final version of your loan application, confirming that all the information provided is accurate and up-to-date.
7. **HUD-1 Settlement Statement**: In some cases, you may receive a HUD-1 settlement statement, which provides a detailed breakdown of all the costs associated with the sale. This document is similar to the closing disclosure and is used primarily for cash transactions or certain types of loans.

It's important to review each document carefully before signing. If you have any questions or concerns, don't hesitate to ask your attorney or your REALPRO agent for clarification. Remember, these documents are legally binding, so it's essential to understand what you're agreeing to.

What to Expect During the Closing Meeting

The closing meeting typically takes place at the office of the title company, escrow agent, or attorney handling the transaction. It usually involves the buyer, seller, real estate agents, and possibly the lender and attorney. Here's what you can expect during the closing meeting:

1. **Verification of Identity**: You'll need to provide a government-issued photo ID, such as a driver's license or passport, to verify your identity. Make sure to bring two forms of identification, as some title companies or lenders may require this.

2. **Review of Documents**: The closing agent will review each document with you, explaining its purpose and ensuring that you understand what you're signing. Take your time to read through the documents and ask any questions you may have.
3. **Signing the Documents**: Once you've reviewed the documents, you'll sign each one where indicated. The closing agent will guide you through the process, ensuring that everything is signed and notarized correctly.
4. **Payment of Closing Costs**: You'll need to provide payment for the closing costs, either by certified check or wire transfer. Make sure you've arranged this with your bank ahead of time, as wire transfers can take a few hours to process.
5. **Transfer of Ownership**: After all the documents are signed and the closing costs are paid, the title company or attorney will record the deed and mortgage with the local government, officially transferring ownership of the property to you.
6. **Receiving the Keys**: Once the transfer of ownership is complete, you'll receive the keys to your new home! This is the moment you've been waiting for—congratulations, you're now a homeowner!

Consider the experience of Malik and Jasmine, who were closing on their first home. They were initially nervous about the closing process, but their REALPRO agent and attorney guided them through each step, answering their questions and ensuring that everything was in order. By the end of the meeting, they felt confident and excited to start their new chapter as homeowners.

Chapter 12: After the Purchase

Congratulations! You've successfully navigated the homebuying process and are now the proud owner of your new home. But the journey doesn't end there. As a homeowner, you'll have ongoing responsibilities to maintain and protect your investment. In this chapter, we'll explore what to do after the purchase, including moving in, managing home maintenance, and understanding property taxes and insurance.

Moving Into Your New Home

Moving into a new home is an exciting and sometimes overwhelming experience. To make the transition as smooth as possible, it's important to plan ahead and stay organized. Here are some tips to help you settle into your new home:

1. **Create a Moving Checklist**: A moving checklist can help you stay organized and ensure that you don't forget any important tasks. Start by listing everything you need to do before, during, and after the move, such as scheduling movers, transferring utilities, and updating your address.
2. **Transfer Utilities and Services**: Make sure to transfer or set up utilities in your new home, including electricity, gas, water, internet, and trash collection. Schedule the transfer for the day of your move to avoid any interruptions in service.
3. **Change Your Address**: Update your address with the post office, your bank, credit card companies, insurance providers, and any other important contacts. Don't

forget to notify your employer, doctor, and any subscriptions or memberships you have.
4. **Pack Strategically**: When packing, label each box with its contents and the room it belongs in. This will make unpacking much easier and help you find what you need more quickly. Pack an "essentials" box with items you'll need immediately upon arrival, such as toiletries, a change of clothes, and basic kitchen supplies.
5. **Inspect Your New Home**: Before you start unpacking, take a final walk through your new home to ensure everything is in order. Check for any damage or issues that may have occurred during the move and document them with photos.
6. **Meet Your Neighbors**: Introduce yourself to your new neighbors and get to know the community. Building good relationships with your neighbors can enhance your experience in your new home and provide a sense of belonging.
7. **Familiarize Yourself with the Area**: Take some time to explore your new neighborhood and locate important places such as grocery stores, pharmacies, schools, and parks. Getting to know the area will help you feel more at home and make it easier to navigate your new surroundings.

Consider the experience of Alejandro and Carla, who recently moved into their new home with their two young children. To make the move easier, they created a detailed moving checklist and labeled each box with the room it belonged in. They also scheduled their utilities to be transferred on the day of the move and packed an essentials box with everything they needed for the first night. By planning ahead, they were able to settle into their new home quickly and comfortably.

Managing Home Maintenance

Owning a home comes with ongoing responsibilities, including regular maintenance and repairs. Proper home maintenance is essential to preserving the value of your property and ensuring that your home remains safe and comfortable. Here are some tips for managing home maintenance:

1. **Create a Maintenance Schedule**: A maintenance schedule can help you stay on top of routine tasks and prevent small issues from becoming major problems. Your schedule should include tasks such as changing HVAC filters, cleaning gutters, inspecting the roof, and servicing the heating and cooling systems. Many tasks can be done seasonally, so it's helpful to create a checklist for each season.
2. **Budget for Repairs**: It's important to set aside money for home repairs and unexpected maintenance. A good rule of thumb is to budget 1% to 3% of your home's value each year for maintenance and repairs. For example, if your home is valued at $300,000, you should budget between $3,000 and $9,000 annually.
3. **Keep Records of Maintenance**: Keep a record of all maintenance and repairs performed on your home, including receipts, warranties, and contractor information. This documentation can be valuable if you decide to sell your home in the future, as it shows that the property has been well-maintained.

4. **Address Issues Promptly**: Don't ignore maintenance issues, even if they seem minor. Small problems, such as a leaky faucet or a cracked window, can lead to larger, more expensive repairs if left unaddressed. Taking care of issues promptly will save you time, money, and stress in the long run.
5. **Hire Professionals When Needed**: While many maintenance tasks can be done yourself, some jobs require the expertise of a professional. Don't hesitate to hire a licensed contractor or technician for complex or hazardous tasks, such as electrical work, plumbing repairs, or roof replacements.

For example, consider the case of Sofia and Luis, who purchased an older home with a charming, historic design. They knew that the home would require regular maintenance to preserve its character and functionality. Sofia and Luis created a detailed maintenance schedule and set aside a portion of their budget for repairs. When they noticed that the roof was showing signs of wear, they hired a professional roofing contractor to assess the situation and make the necessary repairs, preventing more significant damage down the road.

Understanding Property Taxes and Insurance

As a homeowner, you'll be responsible for paying property taxes and maintaining adequate homeowners insurance. Both of these expenses are essential to protecting your investment and ensuring that you comply with local regulations.

1. **Property Taxes**: Property taxes are assessed by your local government and are typically based on the assessed value

of your home and the tax rate in your area. Property taxes are used to fund public services such as schools, roads, and emergency services. Property tax bills are usually issued annually or semi-annually, and it's important to pay them on time to avoid penalties. Your lender may require you to include property taxes in your monthly mortgage payment, which they will then pay on your behalf through an escrow account.

2. **Homeowners Insurance**: Homeowners insurance is a type of property insurance that covers losses and damages to your home and personal belongings. It also provides liability coverage in case someone is injured on your property. Most lenders require homeowners insurance as a condition of the mortgage, and it's important to maintain adequate coverage throughout the life of the loan. When choosing a homeowners insurance policy, consider factors such as the coverage limits, deductibles, and any additional endorsements you may need, such as flood or earthquake coverage.

3. **Reviewing Your Policy Annually**: It's a good idea to review your homeowners insurance policy annually to ensure that it still meets your needs. If you've made significant improvements to your home, such as a kitchen remodel or a new roof, you may need to increase your coverage to reflect the increased value of your property. Additionally, if you've paid off your mortgage, you may be able to adjust your coverage or shop around for a better rate.

4. **Appealing Property Taxes**: If you believe that your property has been over-assessed, you may have the option to appeal your property taxes. This involves providing evidence that the assessed value of your home is higher than its actual market value, such as recent comparable sales in your area. Your local tax assessor's office can provide information on the appeals process and any deadlines you need to meet.

For instance, consider the experience of Rachel and David, who received their first property tax bill after moving into their new home. They were surprised to see that the assessed value of their property was higher than they expected. After discussing the situation with their REALPRO agent, they decided to appeal the assessment by providing recent sales data for similar homes in their neighborhood. Their appeal was successful, and their property tax bill was adjusted to a more accurate amount.

In summary, after purchasing your home, it's important to manage your responsibilities as a homeowner, including moving in, maintaining your property, and understanding property taxes and insurance. By staying organized, planning ahead, and addressing issues promptly, you can protect your investment and enjoy your new home for years to come.

Chapter 13: Best Practices for Homebuyers

Buying a home is a significant financial and emotional investment, and following best practices throughout the process can help ensure a smooth and successful experience. Whether you're a first-time buyer or have purchased homes before, it's important to stay organized, avoid common mistakes, and maintain clear communication with your REALPRO agent. In this chapter, we'll explore the best practices for homebuyers, including staying organized, avoiding common pitfalls, and effectively communicating with your agent.

Staying Organized Throughout the Process

The homebuying process involves many steps, documents, and deadlines, and staying organized is key to ensuring that nothing falls through the cracks. Here are some tips for staying organized:

1. **Create a Homebuying Timeline**: A homebuying timeline can help you keep track of important milestones and deadlines, from getting pre-approved for a mortgage to closing on your new home. Your timeline should include key dates such as when to submit your loan application, when to schedule the home inspection, and when to complete the final walkthrough.
2. **Use a Document Checklist**: Keep a checklist of all the documents you'll need throughout the process, such as your pre-approval letter, purchase agreement, inspection report, and closing disclosure. As you receive each

document, check it off your list and keep it in a dedicated folder or digital file for easy access.
3. **Set Up a Filing System**: Create a filing system for all your homebuying documents, both physical and digital. Use labeled folders or a digital cloud storage system to organize your documents by category, such as "Loan Documents," "Property Information," and "Closing Papers." This will make it easy to find what you need when you need it.
4. **Keep Track of Expenses**: Buying a home comes with various expenses, including down payment, closing costs, and moving expenses. Keep a detailed record of all your expenses, and create a budget to ensure that you stay on track. Tracking your expenses can also help you identify areas where you can save money.
5. **Stay on Top of Communication**: Throughout the homebuying process, you'll need to communicate with your REALPRO agent, lender, attorney, and other professionals. Make sure to respond to emails, phone calls, and requests for information promptly to keep the process moving forward.

Consider the experience of Emma and Carlos, who were purchasing their first home. They used a homebuying timeline and document checklist to stay organized, which helped them stay on top of deadlines and ensure that they had all the necessary paperwork. By staying organized, they were able to navigate the process with confidence and avoid any last-minute surprises.

Common Mistakes to Avoid

While buying a home is an exciting experience, it's also easy to make mistakes that can lead to unnecessary stress or financial setbacks. Here are some common mistakes to avoid:

1. **Skipping the Pre-Approval Process**: One of the biggest mistakes homebuyers make is skipping the pre-approval process. Getting pre-approved for a mortgage not only gives you a clear idea of your budget but also shows sellers that you're a serious buyer. Without pre-approval, you risk falling in love with a home that's out of your price range or losing out to other buyers who are pre-approved.
2. **Overextending Your Budget**: It's important to set a realistic budget and stick to it. While it's tempting to stretch your budget to afford a more expensive home, doing so can lead to financial strain down the road. Remember to factor in all the costs of homeownership, including property taxes, insurance, maintenance, and utilities.
3. **Waiving the Home Inspection**: In a competitive market, some buyers may be tempted to waive the home inspection to make their offer more attractive. However, skipping the inspection can be risky, as it leaves you vulnerable to hidden issues that could be costly to repair. Always schedule a thorough home inspection, even if it means negotiating other terms to make your offer stand out.
4. **Making Emotional Decisions**: Buying a home is an emotional process, but it's important to stay objective and make decisions based on facts rather than feelings. Avoid

rushing into a purchase or overpaying for a home simply because you've fallen in love with it. Take the time to evaluate each property carefully and consider how it aligns with your long-term goals.
5. **Changing Your Financial Situation**: Once you've been pre-approved for a mortgage, it's important to avoid making any major changes to your financial situation, such as taking on new debt, changing jobs, or making large purchases. Lenders may re-evaluate your financial situation before closing, and any changes could jeopardize your loan approval.

For example, consider the case of Brian and Rachel, who were excited to buy their first home. After finding the perfect property, they were tempted to waive the home inspection to strengthen their offer. However, their REALPRO agent advised against it, and they proceeded with the inspection. The inspection revealed significant issues with the plumbing and electrical systems, which would have been costly to repair. By avoiding the mistake of skipping the inspection, they were able to negotiate a lower price and avoid unexpected expenses.

How to Communicate Effectively with Your Agent

Clear and consistent communication with your REALPRO agent is essential to a successful homebuying experience. Your agent is your advocate, guide, and resource throughout the process, and maintaining open lines of communication will help ensure that everything goes smoothly. Here are some tips for communicating effectively with your agent:

1. **Set Clear Expectations**: At the beginning of the process, discuss your goals, preferences, and budget with your agent. Let them know what you're looking for in a home, your preferred timeline, and any specific needs or concerns you have. Setting clear expectations from the start will help your agent tailor their search to your needs.
2. **Be Honest and Transparent**: Honesty is key to a successful relationship with your agent. Be upfront about your financial situation, your priorities, and any challenges you're facing. If you have any concerns or reservations about a property, don't hesitate to share them with your agent. They're there to help you make the best decision for your situation.
3. **Respond Promptly**: The homebuying process often involves tight timelines, so it's important to respond to your agent's emails, phone calls, and requests for information as quickly as possible. Delays in communication can lead to missed opportunities or delays in the process.
4. **Ask Questions**: Don't be afraid to ask questions, even if you think they're basic or repetitive. Your agent is there to help you understand the process and make informed decisions. Whether it's a question about the market, a specific property, or the closing process, your agent will appreciate your proactive approach to learning.
5. **Provide Feedback**: After viewing properties, provide your agent with feedback about what you liked and didn't like. This will help them refine their search and find homes that better match your preferences. Similarly, if you're not satisfied with how something is being handled,

communicate your concerns so that your agent can address them.

Consider the experience of Jessica and Michael, who were searching for a home in a competitive market. They made it a point to communicate regularly with their REALPRO agent, providing detailed feedback after each property viewing and responding promptly to any requests. Their clear communication helped their agent understand their needs and find the perfect home quickly, even in a fast-moving market.

In summary, following best practices for homebuyers can help ensure a smooth and successful experience. By staying organized, avoiding common mistakes, and maintaining clear communication with your REALPRO agent, you can navigate the homebuying process with confidence and achieve your goal of homeownership.

Chapter 14: Real Estate in Different Markets

The real estate market is dynamic and varies greatly depending on location, economic conditions, and seasonal trends. Understanding the differences between a buyer's market and a seller's market, as well as how seasonal trends can affect your homebuying experience, is crucial to making informed decisions. In this chapter, we'll explore the characteristics of different markets, how to navigate them, and strategies for buying a home in a competitive market.

Buying in a Seller's Market vs. Buyer's Market

The terms "seller's market" and "buyer's market" describe the balance of power between buyers and sellers in the real estate market. Understanding which type of market you're in can help you tailor your approach to buying a home.

1. **Seller's Market**: A seller's market occurs when there are more buyers than available homes for sale. This high demand gives sellers the upper hand, often leading to higher prices, multiple offers, and homes selling quickly. In a seller's market, buyers may need to act fast and be prepared to make strong, competitive offers to secure a home. It's common to see homes selling for above the asking price, and buyers may need to waive certain contingencies, such as the home inspection or appraisal contingency, to make their offer more attractive.
For example, consider Rosa and Miguel, who were looking to buy a home in a popular neighborhood during a seller's market. They quickly realized that homes were

selling within days of being listed, often with multiple offers. With the guidance of their REALPRO agent, they decided to make an offer that was slightly above the asking price and waived the inspection contingency to make their offer more competitive. While this strategy carried some risk, it ultimately helped them secure the home they loved.

2. **Buyer's Market**: A buyer's market occurs when there are more homes for sale than there are buyers. This gives buyers the upper hand, as sellers may be more willing to negotiate on price, terms, and closing costs to attract offers. In a buyer's market, homes tend to stay on the market longer, and buyers have more options to choose from. This environment allows buyers to take their time, compare properties, and negotiate better deals.

   Let's look at the experience of David and Sofia, who were searching for a home in a buyer's market. With plenty of homes to choose from, they were able to take their time and carefully evaluate each property. When they found a home they liked, they made an offer below the asking price, asking the seller to cover some of the closing costs. Their REALPRO agent helped them negotiate a favorable deal, and they ended up purchasing the home for less than they had initially expected.

Understanding Seasonal Trends

The real estate market is also influenced by seasonal trends, with certain times of the year typically being more active than others. Understanding these trends can help you decide when to start your home search and what to expect in terms of competition and pricing.

1. **Spring and Summer**: Spring and summer are traditionally the busiest seasons for real estate. During these months, more homes are listed for sale, and buyer activity increases. This is often due to the warmer weather, longer daylight hours, and the desire to move before the new school year begins. While the increased inventory provides more options for buyers, it also means more competition, which can drive up prices. If you're buying in the spring or summer, be prepared to move quickly and make competitive offers.
2. **Fall**: The real estate market typically slows down in the fall, as the peak buying season comes to an end. However, this can be a good time to buy, as there may be less competition from other buyers. Sellers who have not sold their homes during the spring or summer may be more motivated to negotiate on price, especially as the holiday season approaches. Fall can offer a good balance of inventory and pricing, making it a favorable time for buyers who are not in a rush.
3. **Winter**: Winter is usually the slowest season for real estate, with fewer homes on the market and fewer buyers actively searching. This slowdown is often due to the holidays, colder weather, and shorter daylight hours. However, buying in the winter can have its advantages. With less competition, buyers may have more negotiating power, and sellers who list their homes in the winter may be more motivated to close the deal quickly. Additionally, home prices in the winter may be lower, as sellers adjust

their pricing to attract buyers during the slower season. For instance, consider the experience of Jasmine and Marcus, who were searching for a home during the winter months. While they found that there were fewer homes to choose from, they also faced less competition from other buyers. They were able to take their time and negotiate a lower price on a home that had been on the market for several months. Their REALPRO agent helped them navigate the winter market and find a great deal.

Buying a Home in a Competitive Market

Buying a home in a competitive market can be challenging, but with the right strategies and guidance from your REALPRO agent, you can increase your chances of success. Here are some tips for standing out in a competitive market:

1. **Get Pre-Approved**: Before you start your home search, get pre-approved for a mortgage. A pre-approval letter shows sellers that you're a serious buyer with the financial backing to close the deal. In a competitive market, being pre-approved can give you an edge over other buyers who have not yet secured financing.
2. **Make a Strong Offer**: In a competitive market, making a strong offer is essential. Your offer should be based on a thorough understanding of the market and comparable sales in the area. Consider offering slightly above the asking price, especially if the property is priced competitively. Your REALPRO agent can help you determine the best offer strategy based on the market conditions.

3. **Limit Contingencies**: While contingencies are important for protecting your interests, in a competitive market, limiting contingencies can make your offer more attractive to sellers. For example, you might consider waiving the inspection contingency if you're confident in the property's condition. However, be cautious about waiving contingencies, as it can increase your risk.
4. **Be Flexible with Closing Terms**: Flexibility can make your offer stand out in a competitive market. If the seller needs a quick closing or prefers to stay in the home for a few extra weeks after closing, consider accommodating their timeline. Your willingness to be flexible can make your offer more appealing.
5. **Include a Personal Letter**: In some cases, including a personal letter with your offer can help you connect with the seller on an emotional level. The letter should express your appreciation for the home and explain why it's the perfect fit for you and your family. While this strategy may not work in all situations, it can make a difference in a competitive market.

Consider the experience of Emily and Daniel, who were searching for a home in a highly competitive market. With the guidance of their REALPRO agent, they got pre-approved for a mortgage and made a strong offer on a home that had just been listed. To stand out, they waived the inspection contingency and included a personal letter to the seller. Their strategy paid off, and their offer was accepted over several others.

Chapter 15: Working with REALPRO for Your Next Home

Your relationship with REALPRO doesn't end after you've purchased your home. Whether you're planning to sell your current home, buy an investment property, or relocate to a new area, REALPRO's commitment to customer satisfaction extends well beyond the initial transaction. In this chapter, we'll explore how REALPRO can assist you with your future real estate needs, the process of selling your home with REALPRO, and the long-term support and resources available to you as a REALPRO client.

Selling Your Home with REALPRO

When the time comes to sell your home, whether it's to upgrade, downsize, or relocate, working with a REALPRO agent can help you achieve the best possible outcome. Selling a home involves many steps, from setting the right price to marketing the property and negotiating offers. Your REALPRO agent will guide you through the entire process, ensuring that your home sells quickly and for the highest possible price.

1. **Setting the Right Price**: One of the most important factors in selling your home is setting the right price. Pricing your home too high can deter potential buyers, while pricing it too low can leave money on the table. Your REALPRO agent will conduct a comparative market analysis (CMA) to determine the fair market value of your home. This analysis considers recent sales of similar properties in your area, the condition of your home, and current market

trends. Based on this information, your agent will help you set a competitive price that attracts buyers while maximizing your return.

2. **Preparing Your Home for Sale**: First impressions matter, and preparing your home for sale can make a significant difference in how quickly it sells and the price it commands. Your REALPRO agent will provide you with recommendations for staging your home, making minor repairs, and enhancing its curb appeal. This might include decluttering, repainting, landscaping, and addressing any maintenance issues. In some cases, your agent may suggest professional staging to highlight your home's best features.

3. **Marketing Your Home**: Effective marketing is key to reaching the right buyers and generating interest in your home. REALPRO agents use a variety of marketing strategies to showcase your property, including professional photography, virtual tours, online listings, social media promotion, and open houses. Your agent will create a customized marketing plan that targets potential buyers and highlights the unique features of your home.

4. **Negotiating Offers**: Once your home is on the market, you may receive multiple offers from interested buyers. Your REALPRO agent will help you evaluate each offer, considering factors such as the offered price, contingencies, and the buyer's financing. Your agent will also handle negotiations with the buyer's agent to ensure that you get the best possible terms. Whether it's negotiating a higher price, adjusting the closing timeline,

or addressing contingencies, your agent will work to protect your interests throughout the process.

5. **Closing the Sale**: After accepting an offer, your REALPRO agent will guide you through the closing process, coordinating with the buyer's agent, the title company, and your attorney to ensure a smooth transaction. Your agent will help you prepare for the closing, review the final documents, and ensure that all conditions of the sale are met. Once the sale is complete, your agent will be there to answer any questions and provide support as you transition to your next home.

For example, consider the experience of Clara and Javier, who decided to sell their home to move closer to family. With the help of their REALPRO agent, they set a competitive price, made some minor improvements to the property, and launched a targeted marketing campaign. The home received multiple offers within the first week, and their agent helped them navigate the negotiations to secure the best possible deal. The sale closed smoothly, and Clara and Javier were able to move on to their next chapter with confidence.

REALPRO's Commitment to Customer Satisfaction

At REALPRO, customer satisfaction is at the heart of everything we do. Our agents are dedicated to providing exceptional service, not just during the transaction but long after the deal is done. Whether you're a first-time homebuyer or a seasoned investor, REALPRO is committed to supporting you throughout your real estate journey.

1. **Ongoing Support**: Even after you've purchased or sold a home, your REALPRO agent is available to assist you with any real estate-related needs. Whether you have questions about property taxes, need recommendations for contractors, or want to explore refinancing options, your agent is just a phone call or email away. REALPRO's commitment to long-term relationships means that we're here to help you at every stage of homeownership.
2. **Access to Resources**: As a REALPRO client, you have access to a wealth of resources to help you manage and protect your real estate investment. This includes market updates, home maintenance tips, and information on refinancing, home equity loans, and other financial products. REALPRO's website also offers tools for tracking property values, researching neighborhoods, and staying informed about local market trends.
3. **Investment Opportunities**: If you're interested in expanding your real estate portfolio, REALPRO can assist you with identifying and evaluating investment opportunities. Whether you're looking to purchase a rental property, flip a home, or invest in commercial real estate, your REALPRO agent can provide guidance on market conditions, financing options, and property management.
4. **Relocation Services**: If you're relocating to a new area, REALPRO's network of agents can help you find the perfect home in your new location. Whether you're moving across town or across the country, your REALPRO agent can connect you with a trusted local agent who knows the area and can assist with your home search. We'll also help coordinate the sale of your current home

and the purchase of your new home, making your move as seamless as possible.

How REALPRO Supports You in the Long Term

REALPRO's commitment to your success extends beyond the transaction. We're dedicated to helping you achieve your real estate goals, whether that means selling your home, purchasing an investment property, or managing your real estate portfolio. Here's how REALPRO supports you in the long term:

1. **Building a Long-Term Relationship**: At REALPRO, we believe in building long-term relationships with our clients. Your agent will take the time to understand your evolving needs and provide personalized service that grows with you. Whether you're buying your first home, upsizing for a growing family, or planning for retirement, your REALPRO agent will be there to guide you every step of the way.
2. **Navigating Future Transactions**: As your real estate needs change over time, your REALPRO agent will be there to assist with future transactions. Whether you're buying a vacation home, selling an investment property, or relocating to a new area, your agent will provide expert guidance and support to ensure a successful outcome.
3. **Achieving Your Real Estate Goals**: REALPRO is committed to helping you achieve your long-term real estate goals. Whether that means building wealth through real estate investments, creating a legacy for your family, or finding your dream home, your agent will work with you to

develop a strategy that aligns with your goals and supports your financial future.

For instance, consider the experience of Luis and Maria, who purchased their first home with the help of a REALPRO agent. Over the years, they worked with their agent to buy an investment property, sell their first home, and purchase a larger home for their growing family. Throughout each transaction, their REALPRO agent provided expert advice, market insights, and personalized service, helping them achieve their real estate goals and build a secure financial future.

Buying A Home?
Visit www.realprointernational.com
scan below

Or call
1-855-310-HOME

www.ingramcontent.com/pod-product-compliance
Lightning Source LLC
Chambersburg PA
CBHW070355230526
45471CB00006B/2581